SARAH RA̶̶̶̶ ̶̶̶̶̶̶

More
Making Friends
with Anxiety

**A little book of creative activities
to help reduce worry and panic**

With drawings and photos
by the author

Also by Sarah Rayner

The 'Making Friends' series:

Making Friends with Anxiety: A warm, supportive little book to help ease worry and panic

Making Friends with Anxiety:
A Calming Colouring Book

Making Friends with Depression:
A warm and wise companion to recovery

Making Friends with the Menopause: A clear and comforting guide to support you as your body changes

Fiction:

Another Night, Another Day
The Two Week Wait
One Moment, One Morning
Getting Even
The Other Half

ISBN: 978-1523302413

www.sarah-rayner.com

Hello and welcome

I'm **Sarah Rayner**, an author. Some of you may know my novels, which include *One Moment, One Morning* and *The Two Week Wait*. Or you might have come across my non-fiction titles, *Making Friends with Anxiety: A warm, supportive little book to help ease worry and panic*, or *Making Friends with Anxiety: A Calming Colouring Book*. If you liked those, I hope you'll enjoy this too, but it works equally well as a standalone read.

'Isn't it unusual for a novelist to write about anxiety?' I hear you ask. So I'll explain what drew me to the subject, and to use arts and crafts as therapy too.

When it comes to anxiety, *I've been there*. I've suffered from bad bouts of panic and fear, so I know how debilitating and distressing it can be. Whilst I've not *cured* my anxiety (that would be an over-claim for any person or book to make), I have learned how to manage my inclination to excessive worry. I found that understanding the emotion and physical symptoms gave me the ability to live with it.

Whereas, hitherto, panic and fear had often controlled me, these days you could say that anxiety occupies a space in my life rather like an annoying flatmate; one who doesn't do the washing up or put the loo seat down. My anxiety gremlin is there; he can't always be ignored, and some days he really irks me, but he doesn't really do me any harm, or curtail how I choose to spend my time.

This was a breakthrough for me, and a huge relief. I felt freed up and happier. Then, because I've written a lot of guides (for 20 years I was an advertising copywriter), I thought I might be able to help others by sharing my experiences and explaining what worked (and didn't work) for me. This led me to pen the first *Making Friends with Anxiety* book, and now I'm delighted to expand on what I've learned in this little follow-up book. *More Making Friends with Anxiety* contains further in-depth advice on reducing stress and worry and many new tips on anxiety management. It's offset by some of my drawings and photos, including pictures of things I've made.

Designed to lift your spirits

This leads me onto the creative aspect of the book. I might be a writer by trade, but I've been making things since I was small. Painting, sewing, gardening, potting, baking – the list goes on. As well as being a form of self-expression and highly enjoyable, I've found many of these pastimes comforting, so when I've been anxious, it's to gentle activities like these that I naturally turn. This drawing of my stepson Sebastian, for example, I drew a few years ago when I was feeling very wobbly indeed.

SR

Whilst this particular pastel picture turned out OK, rest assured many of my creative endeavours have not been especially successful – I've made fudge that hasn't set, planted seeds that haven't grown, and strung necklaces that have snapped. I admit this not because I want you to worry that the instructions that follow will result in failure, but because **I don't**

5

want you to think that any of the creative pursuits in this book are beyond you. *More Making Friends with Anxiety* is not just for those who consider themselves arty and crafty already – *it's for anyone who wants to be more creative and less stressed.* Together we'll take a closer look at 10 gentle, hands-on activities that I've chosen because they're fun and easy. If you're one of the millions of adults who have enjoyed colouring books and found them calming, this little book gives you the chance to experiment with different crafts and see if they too can help improve your state of mind.

Perhaps you've not done much gardening before, in which case you can discover how to plant a window box, or maybe you'd like to try whittling wood or making a collage, so you can still be creative even if it's wet and you're stuck indoors. But whether you're stitching a mobile phone cover, painting a pebble or carving a spoon from wood, it isn't my intention for you to feel as if you're being given a lesson or completing a task. I don't want you to be intimidated or concerned that you're not skilled enough. Nor do I wish you, dear reader, to get caught up in making something perfect.

You might like to try the activities alone, or with a friend or family member. Many of the activities are well suited to be done with children. Yet whoever you're with, **the idea is to focus on what you are doing without worrying too much about the result.** Then you should find yourself in an almost meditative state – and that's the first step to easing worry and panic right there.

The healing power of gentle, creative activities

We'll also look at *why* occupying ourselves in certain ways can be so therapeutic, examining the effect various creative activities have upon the mind and body. **I'll explore the link between mental and physical symptoms and explain how the** simple act of making something can play a valuable role in de-stressing from the day-to-day grind.

Here it's helpful to clarify that broadly speaking 'anxiety' and 'stress' are two different words to describe the same physical experience – the symptoms of a higher heart rate, sweaty palms, churning stomach and so on. The main difference is that anxiety is usually seen as short-term, whereas stress can last for weeks, months, even years. However, the effects on the body and mind are similar, so by tackling the symptoms of anxiety using the approach in this book, you'll also tackle the symptoms of stress. Although of course you don't *have* to be stressed to have a go at the activities – there's plenty to enjoy about being creative if you're on an even keel.

Whilst I'm on the subject of symptoms, **it's only fair to point out here at the start that if you've read either of the other two *Making Friends with Anxiety* books you may notice one or two overlaps in terms of content.** Because I want new readers to have access to the tools I've found invaluable in managing my own anxiety, I believe that it's important to include this information again, but if you're already familiar with the relationship between anxiety and adrenaline, for instance, you might like to skip or skim read Chapter 1. Personally I feel that I can never be reminded too often of the physical aspects of anxiety, as it's quite easy to forget them when we're caught in a mental whirl of worry, but I leave it with you to decide.

Expert tips and insights

In addition, interspersed throughout the text are **tried-and-tested tips from members of the** *Making Friends with Anxiety Facebook Group,* many of whom have acquired great wisdom as a result of their own experience of fear and panic. The group was founded to provide a space for anxiety sufferers to share experiences and support one another in confidence and now has several thousand members. If you'd like to join, we're at **www.facebook.com/groups/makingfriendswithanxiety/.**

Ultimately, **how you use this book is up to you. You might choose to just read the advice on anxiety management for now, and then come back and do one or two of the creative activities another day. Or you might like to work your way through all the activities from beginning to end.** But whatever journey *More Making Friends with Anxiety* takes you on, I hope this little book provides you with insight and inspiration, and many hours of pleasure.

Sarah

Contents

Chapter 1. Anxiety affects us all
So why is anxiety a problem?
What happens physically when we experience anxiety?
Fear is natural and useful
How do we befriend anxiety?
Try not to focus so much on the future
Stop overthinking everything
Make contact with nature
Exercise – but do what you enjoy
Kiss good-bye to strict diets

Chapter 2. How creativity helps mental and physical health
What makes particular pursuits so therapeutic?
The reduction of adrenaline
Doing something with our hands as a displacement activity
Forming a crafting circle
Not all creative pursuits are equally calming

Chapter 3. Glass painting – helping boost fragile confidence
Drawing on therapeutic tradition
Painting teaches us to 'own' our mistakes
Getting started
- You will need
- How to paint a simple glass vase
- How to paint a patterned tea-light holder
- Deciding on your design
- Which colours to choose?

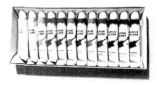

Chapter 4. Painting pebbles – a gentle way to face fear

Venturing into the unknown

Anxiety and agoraphobia

Avoidance tactics

Overcoming fear

Step by step

Getting started

- How to paint a pebble
- You will need
- Instructions
- Ways to use your finished stones

Chapter 5. Collage – the joy of letting rip

What is collage?

Collage is free and fun

Almost anything can be used

Collage brings words and pictures together

Getting started

- Make a 'mantra' collage using a quote you like
- Instructions
- Keep a collage journal

Chapter 6. Needlework – 'active' meditation made easy

Busy hands, healthy mind

Playing with pattern

A balanced approach

Getting started

- Sew your own mobile phone cover
- You will need
- Instructions

Chapter 7. Whittling – honing objects to use every day

What is whittling?

Getting started

- How to carve a spoon
- You will need
- Instructions

Chapter 8. Container gardening – at one with Mother Nature

Getting started

- How to plant a window box
- Instructions

Chapter 9. Sowing from seed – growing yourself better

Why gardening is such good therapy?

Getting started

- Growing summer flowers from seed
- Instructions

Chapter 10. Baking – making magic in the kitchen

Baking and body-consciousness

Don't beat yourself up

Whatever you knead

Sweet versus savoury

Considerations whatever you choose to make

Getting started

- How to make a blackberry and apple crumble
- Go blackberry picking
- Ingredients
- Method

Chapter 11. Making jewellery – learning to love ourselves

Becoming more confident

Creating something precious

Getting started

       How to make an endless beaded necklace

       You will need

       Instructions

Chapter 12. Looking and listening – appreciating other people's creativity

Think you're not creative?

Why looking at art is good for our mental health

Listening to music

Thank you

About Sarah Rayner

Non-fiction by Sarah Rayner

Fiction by Sarah Rayner

Useful websites

Recommended reading

Related articles

Chapter 1. Anxiety affects us all

Let's kick off with an assertion: that you, dear reader, are anxious. I can say this not just because this book has got 'anxiety' in the title and you're choosing to read it, but because *everyone* is anxious in some way.

'But I know lots of people who never seem to worry about anything,' you might counter. 'They sail through life with a la di da and nothing ever fazes them.' I get where you're coming from. Take someone like the Dalai Lama – he seems a very mellow fellow, so how can I make such a sweeping statement? Admittedly, I've no idea if the Dalai Lama tosses and turns at night or bites his nails in secret, but I'd still assert that His Holiness experiences anxiety. Moreover, there's nothing wrong with this. This is because **anxiety is as common and natural an emotion as happiness and sadness, love and compassion**. So unless the Dalai Lama simply isn't human, he'll experience anxiety to some degree, and I don't know about you, but I find just knowing this is comforting.

So why is anxiety a problem?

Actually, it's not anxiety that's the problem, it's that some people experience *heightened* **anxiety.** Sometimes we feel it in sudden flashes, which can result in panic attacks. Or we can find ourselves going through a period of ongoing stress and suffer symptoms often associated with that – an upset stomach, headaches and insomnia.

To feel stressed is very common: a recent survey by the Mental Health Foundation found that nearly 50% of workers struggle to switch off from their jobs, and nearly two thirds of people are keen to take part in activities that might help them unwind. And whilst I'm nowhere near as bad as I was – when I was at my worst, on some days I was pinned to the floor by anxiety – I'd still put myself in The Worrywart Club even today. You can probably place yourself somewhere on a scale which has me close to one end and our Tibetan friend at the other.

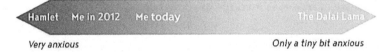

Very anxious   Only a tiny bit anxious

'Therein lies the rub,' as Hamlet (who knew a thing or two about fretting) would say. If anxiety is a perfectly natural emotion, why does it dominate the lives of some of us in particular? **Panic attacks, OCD, Post Traumatic Stress – however it manifests itself, anxiety can be very distressing when we're in its thrall.**

The reasons that an individual can end up caught in the cycle of panic tend to be complex – some adults and children simply seem to be more sensitive and *feel* more deeply, others may find themselves whacked by a series of distressing circumstances in close succession. Sometimes a major event such as redundancy or bereavement will be the trigger. And to compound this, it is widely acknowledged that we live in a particularly anxiety-provoking age where work emails and social networking and worries about debt and climate-change jostle for our headspace 24/7. But whilst I'm sure our modern lifestyle has a large part to play in why many of us feel near crazy a lot of the time, and of course it's helpful to understand the psychological roots of anxiety, neither is going to be the focus of this book. As almost anyone anxious will tell you, it is immediate relief they're after, and debating whether it's nature or nurture that's responsible for the onset of symptoms would only detract from that.

Instead I'll share as succinctly and clearly as possible what I found most useful when it came to managing my own anxiety in the hope this will help you. Then in Chapter 2 we'll discover more about the healing powers of arts, crafts and creativity.

What happens physically when we experience anxiety?

It might surprise you to discover that anxiety isn't a bad thing per se. In many ways it can actually serve us. This is because anxiety is connected to fear. It could be said that **anxiety is the biological vestige of fear, the basic survival mechanism that helps safeguard us against danger**. When we experience fear, we get a rush of adrenaline.

- **The brain sends a biochemical message saying 'all systems go!'** and our breathing becomes faster and shallower, supplying more oxygen to the muscles.
- **Our hearts beat more rapidly and blood is driven to the brain and limbs** so we can make split-second decisions and a quick getaway. This is why when we are anxious we often experience heart palpitations, chest pains and tingling.
- **Blood is taken from areas of the body where it is not needed**, such as the stomach, because in a life-threatening situation, you're not going to stop for food. So when you're afraid, you may well feel sick and unable to eat.
- **The liver releases stored sugar to provide fuel for quick energy**. Excess sugar in the blood can cause indigestion.
- **Muscles in the anus and bladder are relaxed**. Food and liquid are evacuated so you're lighter in order to run. Hence diarrhoea and frequent urination.
- **The body cools itself by perspiring.** Blood vessels and capillaries move close to the skin surface, leading to sweating and blushing.

Thus what can seem like horribly frightening symptoms are actually normal biological reactions – the same reactions our ancestors have had for thousands of years.

Fear is natural and useful

Fear is natural, that's fact number one. Fact number two is that we need fear, no matter how horrible it feels to be afraid.
Imagine you were being threatened by an aggressive animal. Here the burst of adrenaline would bring about a much-needed 'fight or flight' response, useful if you needed to escape from a hungry lion.

We can often see our pets exhibit these responses. This very morning, when our cat clapped eyes on the basket in which he goes to the vet, he bolted out of the cat flap faster than a horse on Derby day, and he's not normally a swift mover, take it from me. Fear prompted flight, and it took an awful lot of patience (and a sachet of Whiskas) to lure him back inside.

Whilst you might not encounter hungry lions on a daily basis, the good thing about anxiety is it can help alert us to the fact we might be taking too much on and that we have to look after ourselves. So **we need anxiety, just as we need laughter and tears and friends and family; it keeps us safe and healthy.**

The bad thing is that in some of us, fear gets triggered very easily, resulting in too much adrenaline, and an ongoing anxious state of mind – that Hamlet-like headspace I mentioned. Anxiety is the body signalling something is not quite right, and if we experience this series of reactions in a normal situation such as in a supermarket or business meeting, it can be very frightening. **We then become afraid of certain situations and people, and often end up creating a vicious circle where we avoid many things because they trigger what we interpret as a negative reaction.** I'll come back to the subject of avoidance in Chapter 4.

TIP: 'If I feel wound up, I go for a walk. It seems to use up my adrenaline, and after a while the brain seems to clear and problems don't feel so overwhelming.' **Peter**

How do we befriend anxiety?

It was on a course on anxiety management that I finally grasped that anxiety was a natural response, so that to try and banish it from my life was as futile as trying to get rid of my appetite or ability to sneeze. I now understand that it is as much a part of me as they are. But it wasn't always this way. Like many people, I concluded anxiety was what was stopping me from being happy and fulfilled, so I fought it, seeing it as the enemy.

Without wanting to sound evangelical or simplistic, if you suffer from excess worry, high levels of stress or panic attacks, I firmly believe that befriending anxiety is *the* key to feeling better. Fighting anxiety, or avoiding trigger situations won't help in the long run. At its most basic, this means changing our mind-set from one of resistance to one of acceptance. It's not always easy to change how we think, but here are five ways to manage anxiety that you can start implementing today:

1. Try not to focus so much on the future

I've noticed many members of the Facebook group expend a lot of mental energy fearing what is yet to happen, and I have the same tendency. Going back to work in a week's time, meeting the in-laws in a fortnight, having to fly next month – if you're prone to anxiety, I'm sure you can fill in your own panic-provoking scenarios. Yet most are beyond our control and worrying serves no purpose other than to trigger adrenaline and lots of physical symptoms. Personally, I find it impossible not to worry at all, but when I have lots to do, I break my anxieties down into a list of what I have to accomplish on that day and NO MORE THAN THAT. I ignore everything else and tell myself to deal with tomorrow when it arrives.

2. Stop over-thinking everything

To help achieve this, I channel my inner cat – but channelling your inner dog, guinea pig or mouse will do just as well. This isn't as bonkers as it sounds. When other mammals experience fear and have a rush of adrenaline, they don't analyse their symptoms – a cat being chased by a large dog doesn't pause to evaluate 'why is Buster being so aggressive, is it something I've done?' He just high-tails it. At its simplest, this is because our pets live in the present. A cat is happy: it purrs. A dog wants you to throw a ball: it runs up, wagging its tail. Neither creature (unless I'm missing something) is worried about work on Monday. They are as they are. Hungry, playful, hot, sleepy. They express it and move on. If we follow their example and let go of ruminating on the past and worrying about the future and focus on the here and now, anxiety lessens.

TIP: 'Talk to your anxiety in a positive way, as if you are greeting your friend. I do it and as I chat, I can feel my physical symptoms ease. If I build on this positive reaction, it's amazing how quickly my anxiety settles.' **Ellen**

TIP: 'I've got a donkey! When that doubting voice is nagging away, I pretend that it's the donkey from Shrek. I picture him sitting on my shoulder and he makes me smile.' **Alan**

3. Make contact with nature

Every day, take five minutes to experience the great outdoors. Wherever you are, be unashamedly sensual – smell the flowers, gaze at the sky, touch the dewy grass, listen to the birds. Again, this will bring you into the present moment.

4. Kiss good-bye to strict diets

Unless you've an issue with obesity, if you experience heightened anxiety, I think it's a good idea to give up giving up until you're on a more even keel. The symptoms of anxiety will ease gradually if you learn to manage it. Meanwhile, stop dieting, and you'll avoid all that resentment and self-reproach that often goes with counting calories or weighing yourself all the time. Keeping your blood sugar levels stable and avoiding too much caffeine and alcohol will help your anxiety no end, but I believe 'a little bit of what you fancy' doesn't do much harm. One latte a day is probably OK; five isn't. Same with chocolate and cake, coke, wine and beer. Balance is key.

5. Exercise – but do what you enjoy

Physical exercise helps anxiety as it uses up adrenaline and encourages the production of happy hormones. But there's no point joining a gym just because magazines or well-meaning friends tell you to, because if you don't use your membership this will merely create anxiety and guilt. You're better off gardening or dancing or walking the dog. Are you noticing a theme here…? It's called *Do What Makes You Happy*.

TIP: 'When I wobble, I remind myself: this too will pass.' **Carole**

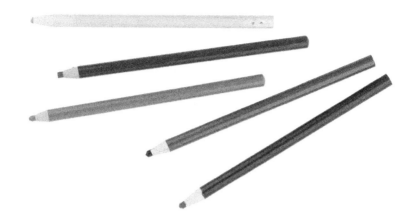

Chapter 2. How creativity helps mental and physical health

'Whilst I love making things, looking back, my creativity was born out of boredom and loneliness,' says designer Cath Newell. 'The long summer holidays, when my brothers would amuse themselves with complex war games, had me opening my cupboards to explore the boxes of craft kits given to me as gifts. It was not long before my bedroom became a confusion of spider plants in hanging macramé baskets, my soft toys all proudly wore wonky knitted scarves and my bean-bag frog collection had spilled over my bookcase.'

Cath now runs workshops for those who want to enjoy being creative together (and overleaf is a photo from her Christmas wreath-making morning). But Cath is not alone in being galvanized into creativity by self-soothing; to a large extent, I, too, was a child who sought refuge in creativity. That Cath and I are lucky enough to have made some sort of living out of our creativity is probably not a coincidence; it's because we've spent so many thousands of hours writing, drawing and making things that there's nothing else we can do as well!

CN

Of course **you don't need to be a professional to enjoy crafts**. In the *Making Friends with Anxiety* group on Facebook, numerous members report that they find being creative beneficial, and many work in completely unrelated fields. The group wall is chock-full of incredibly detailed Zentangles, imaginatively-iced cakes, lovingly-tended gardens, carefully-stitched samplers and expressive paintings. Last Christmas one of our group administrators, Karen, posted photos of some gorgeous felt decorations she'd hand-stitched for her tree, and recently there has been a flurry of people posting pictures they have coloured in *Making Friends with Anxiety: A Calming Colouring Book*.

What makes particular pursuits so therapeutic?

Although these activities may seem to have little in common, in fact many offer similar benefits to anxiety sufferers.

Participating in simple **activities that involve using our hands enable us to stop focusing on the past** (which is often associated with depression) **and the future** (a tendency of the over-anxious) **and be in the here and now**. An activity such

24

as icing a cake like the ones below is not a passive act: we need to make active decisions about which food colourings to use and what shapes to sculpt. The same is true of planting a window box: **the mind is filled with an activity and when we are in what some psychologists call 'the zone' or 'flow' and are fully immersed in what we are doing, we are unable to dissect or churn over anything else.**

'Whether it's sewing a bag, renovating some furniture or making a Christmas wreath, my mind is focused on the task, the materials, the challenges, the journey and finally, usually, great pleasure in having made something that is really appreciated.' **Cath**

This single-mindedness arises because, contrary to common belief, it isn't possible to think of two things at exactly the same time. Instead what happens when we 'multitask' is that the mind darts from one to another, and it is this which leaves us feeling frazzled and intellectually dissatisfied. In contrast, **repetitive creative work can be calming.** This is particularly true if you accept the process as having no expected outcome other than enjoyment and stay open to whatever emerges – though I appreciate this isn't always easy, especially when you are baking a cake!

The reduction of adrenaline

In addition to helping to change our patterns of thinking, **focusing on making something can have a positive impact on us physically as it helps to reduce production of adrenaline.** As our brains become less charged-up, so our bodies become more relaxed, and relaxation lowers the activity of the amygdala, a part of the brain that is affected by stress. Thus many of the physical responses that stem from the release of adrenaline are diminished when we focus on being gently creative: **heart rate slows, breathing becomes less frenetic, blood flows to the stomach so food can be digested more easily** – the list goes on. When we become calmer physically, so our thinking becomes less panicky, and we thereby **turn the vicious circle where anxiety begets more anxiety into a benign one that promotes calm.**

> TIP: *'Remember nothing lasts forever, including anxiety. Even if it can seem as if you will never feel good again, bad times will pass, because every emotion is temporary.'* **Lucy**

Doing something with our hands as a displacement activity

Psychologists sometimes use the term 'displacement activities' to describe motor behaviours that discharge tension or anxiety. Someone in a dentist's waiting room anticipating a cavity filling might scratch his head, stroke his beard, wring his hands, tug at his earlobe or flip through a magazine at speed, for example. It's easy to see how arts and crafts might fulfil a similar role. **When we're anxious about something – be it dental discomfort or a train delay – if we can redirect that nervous energy by occupying our hands elsewhere, it can help to calm**

26

us. But whereas the scratching of one's head or tugging of an earlobe doesn't result in anything – they are 'empty gestures' if you like – embroidering a piece of material or sketching a design idea does. Instead of feeling we're wasting time, we end up with something tangible, and that keeps frustration at bay and lifts mood.

This brings to mind the day of my stepfather's funeral several years ago. Adrian was much loved by many, including my then small nieces and nephew. But whereas we adults directed our grief into conversation, tears and laughter, the children did something quite different.

The morning of the service I came down the stairs of my mother's home to find all four of them busy drawing in the kitchen. Countless cards lay propped up on the table, each inscribed with a different message. 'You waer my best grandad' said one, with a picture of Adrian in his death bed. 'Biy biy card for Adrion', said another, alongside a felt-tip illustration of his grave. I can think of no finer example of 'art therapy', and it struck me how the children seemed to know intuitively that it would help.

Forming a crafting circle

Whilst it's good to spend time alone occasionally, being with other people can decrease the solipsism associated with anxiety. **Fundamental to maintaining a healthy mind is staying engaged with the world outside of ourselves,** because it's all too easy when we're left to mull, for our minds to start whirling in a way that isn't helpful. Of course some people aren't helpful to be around either – if you find certain friends or relatives tend to bring you down, try to spend less time with them, or make sure you encounter them when others are also around so as to reduce the impact.

Instead, seek out and cultivate relationships with those who are positive and appreciate you and share similar interests. To this end, you might like to consider starting 'a crafting circle'. If this sounds a bit fancy, it isn't – **a crafting circle is simply group of like-minded souls** connected by their enjoyment of an activity. Your circle could be made up of people who enjoy sewing, beading, colouring or whittling wood – you name it. Age, sex and ability needn't matter.

Crafting circles are a way to

- Swap tips
- Share tools and materials
- Support one another
- Relax

'In my sewing group we tend to dip in and out of chatting as and when what we are making allows. Conversation seems to flow more easily as a result; perhaps it is because the pressure is off.' **Sally**

How you set up your circle is up to you – just **make sure there is enough room to spread out your materials, enough time together to make something and enough food and drink to sustain you while you work.** You might like to rotate who hosts your circle or try out different creative activities. If you aim to meet once a month, you could even work your way through all the different activities I suggest in this book. Then in less than a year you could have had a go at them all!

Not all creative pursuits are equally calming

With luck all this has made you keen to get started, but before we move on it's worth explaining why I've picked the 10 activities I have, or, to put it another way, why so many creative pursuits *aren't* included here.

      Because the aim of this book is to help alleviate stress and anxiety through the use of gentle hands-on activities, **it's important that we focus on occupying ourselves in ways that aren't too tricky**. The last thing I want is trigger more worry, and I'm sure many creative professionals – be they writers, painters, musicians, chefs or actors – will confirm their work *can* be stressful. Often being creative is most scary when we have to start from scratch and face the blank canvas or page – believe me, as an author, I know! For this reason many of the suggestions in this book have a 'start point' already. This makes them less likely to provoke anxiety because **working within boundaries helps us feel safe**. The parameters might be a pebble, a cake tin, or the sides of a window box, but they are there to guide and ground you.

Chapter 3. Glass painting – helping boost fragile confidence

Our first creative projects have obvious parameters because they involve decorating the surfaces of small objects. In this chapter we'll look at painting a glass vase and a tea-light holder and in Chapter 4 we'll have a go at painting pebbles.

However, I'm aware that for some readers painting even a relatively limited area can seem daunting. It may be the first time you've used art materials in years, possibly since your childhood. Perhaps you have a voice in your ear going 'Think you can paint? You never were any good at art at school,' in which case, tell it to 'Shush!' and try to remember that it's only your anxiety gremlin stirring things. Rather than letting your inexperience lead to self-doubt and trepidation, instead look at it this way: far from being out of practice, you're taking the opportunity to indulge in a childlike pleasure – and you're never too old for that!

Painting allows us to feel small, in a good way. There's something reassuring and comforting about picking up pots of brightly-coloured paint and brushes again, especially

31

when our lives are so dominated by screens and mice and keyboards. George Bernard Shaw said, 'we don't stop playing because we grow old, we grow old because we stop playing.'

SR

Drawing on therapeutic tradition

Nevertheless, in our enthusiasm for colouring and being in the moment, let's not kid ourselves that we are the first generation to dream up art therapy. Back in the early 20th century, the great Swiss thinker, Carl Jung, was convinced that drawing might aid self-exploration, and encouraged his patients to experiment with mandalas – designs which use concentric lines and circles and have their origins in India. He saw them as 'the psychological expression of the totality of the self' and since then research has provided some backing for his theory. Infants are born with a desire to look at circles, probably because the ability to seek out circular, face-like stimuli helps them to bond with their care givers. For a baby, a circle will come forward out of a confusing mass of random visual input and be recognized as something known and familiar.

'Painting mandalas on glass takes me away to a world of my own, a dreamy imaginative place where I feel a sense of peace.' Caroline

'When I was feeling really unwell due to stress last year, I was incapable of concentrating for more than a few minutes,' says Vicki Turner, a member of the Facebook group. 'I found I had to focus on the task in hand, and colouring books enabled me to overcome procrastination. By breaking tasks into manageable steps it helped to improve decision making.'

It seems that colouring is good at building self-esteem and confidence as it's something we do in degrees; **it's challenging but not *too* challenging.** Within the boundaries of the inked lines it is possible to be very creative, of course, but because it has that start point I mentioned earlier, the pressure we put ourselves under is reduced. Painting a tea-light or pebble is similar, but it takes a *tiny* bit more courage because the design isn't done already. That said, I believe the rewards are worth it, because by pushing ourselves a little, we can start to gain more faith in our own ability.

'Painting wee things like pebbles and tea-light holders gives me a sense of achievement. I'm not particularly artistic but because they're so small, I feel I can express myself with confidence.' **Danielle**

Danielle speaks for many; one of the reasons people seem to enjoy crafts like painting glass vases and pebbles is that even those who don't perceive themselves to be artistic believe that they can have a go. Plus there's no need to design anything complicated – your painting can be as plain and simple as you like.

Painting teaches us to 'own' our mistakes

Many anxiety sufferers have perfectionist tendencies and this often exacerbates our worry. Using paint means that we have to risk making mistakes; unlike pencil, it cannot be easily erased. It's a great metaphor for everyday life – **nothing is ever perfect; it's how we adjust to mistakes or the unexpected in life that really matters.**

When you begin painting, take a moment to notice if you are getting caught up in judgment and deliberation. If so, quieten your inner critic and try to enjoy the process. That way you can use painting to teach yourself not to rush and to take good care of what is happening in the present.

TIP: 'If I feel anxious before I set about painting, I do a little deep breathing. I breathe in for the count of four, hold my breath for the count of seven and then release for the count of eight. I repeat this a few times until I feel my heartbeat slow. This stops me absorbing the worries of a bad day and allows me to use the disassociation that comes from painting to full advantage. Works for me every time!'
Amanda

Getting started

You will need

- Glassware – a vase and 2-3 tea-light holders
- Paint brushes
- A plate or palette on which to mix paints
- Paints suitable for glass – acrylic enamel paints are widely available, easy to use and do not require heat to set. They are water based, so dry quickly and harden to create a glossy finish

How to paint a simple glass vase

When it comes to your design, I don't want to be prescriptive and cause you to worry about your approach being 'wrong' in some way. If you're feeling at a loss as to where to start, you might like to go for a single colour. The advantage to this is you can then get used to using your materials before trying something more adventurous. Just mix up a shade you really like on your plate using a little water and apply it to the inside of the vase with a brush. You may need to do a second coat, but if you use acrylic paint as I suggest, once dry it will be waterproof, so you can use your vase to display flowers. Blooming marvellous!

How to paint a patterned tea-light holder

Now for something a little more adventurous. Though 'little' is the appropriate word – we're talking about a tea-light holder, my friends.

Deciding on your design

It can be helpful to draw out your pattern on a piece of flat paper first. Here is an idea you might like, and there are more

suggestions on page 47 for painting pebbles that will work on glass, too. Alternatively, you may prefer to let inspiration guide you and paint directly onto the glass, free-flow.

Which colours to use?

TIP: 'Before I start, I sit quietly for a moment to allow my feelings to settle. I then choose a palette instinctively, from the gut, rather than overthinking it. Try not to get caught up in too many instructions. I'd encourage you to trust your instinct and let imagination be your guide.' **Donna**

Whilst certain colours broadly align with specific traits – red is associated with danger, purple with sophistication, brown with ruggedness and so on – personal experiences, upbringing, cultural difference and context all add nuance to what various shades mean to us individually. **We can also use colours to connect with our emotions and opt for particular shades to reflect our mood.**

When you're ready to move onto something more challenging, you could try painting something bigger, or a more detailed pattern or a figurative (by which I mean 'lifelike') picture. But whatever direction you go in, don't be too tough on yourself. Just allow yourself to feel the connection to the timeless human endeavour of putting paint on a surface, and savour being part of that universe.

Chapter 4. Painting pebbles – a gentle way to face fear

If you've discovered you enjoy glass painting, perhaps you'd like to venture into pastures new – or into the great outdoors, at any rate, as that's where you can find the materials for our next creative project – pebble painting.

Venturing into the unknown

'Pebble painting?' you may retort, and I understand your hesitation. Many of you might find it daunting to embark on a new creative enterprise but for others it might be the notion of heading outside that's off-putting. **When we're stressed by all that life seems to be throwing at us already, it's very natural to want to hunker down and protect ourselves by doing what feels familiar and comfortable.**

At times there's nothing wrong with this, of course. The desire to feel safe and cosseted is part of being human – indeed, the need for a secure place where we can eat and sleep is something we share with many, many creatures on this planet and is perfectly healthy and natural instinct.

'The ache for home lives in all of us, the safe place where we can go as we are and not be questioned.' **Maya Angelou**

A longing for security only becomes a problem when we become trapped by fear of what's new and different, and it inhibits our day-to-day freedom. Some people experience such bad anxiety that they may not be able to leave the house, as a few members of the Facebook group would testify. Yet contrary to how it might appear, this isn't because we anxious types are cowardly; it's because we're doing our best to protect ourselves against foreseeable distress. If this sounds like you, I'd urge you to take a few minutes to read on as it may help you shine a light on your own behaviour and manage your anxiety better in the future.

Anxiety and agoraphobia

Many assume that agoraphobia is a fear of open spaces but it's more complex than this. A person with agoraphobia may be scared of leaving their home, as I've mentioned, but also:

- Travelling on public transport
- Uncontrollable social situations
- Going to the supermarket
- Driving on their own
- Being at the airport

…and more. Agoraphobia is a form of anxiety that occurs when someone perceives an environment to be uncomfortable or unsafe and can be accompanied by panic attacks.

Avoidance tactics

To a large extent whether or not you have a medical diagnosis of agoraphobia doesn't matter here. Even if you're someone who is relatively happy going out and about, it's still worth reading on. We've already established that everyone experiences anxiety occasionally and you may well find that gaining a better understanding of your emotional and physical reactions is liberating.

To overcome anxiety, **it can be very tempting to think the solution is to avoid the situations that trigger it**. I've done this myself – ducking out of public speaking, foregoing parties, postponing plane trips – most of us can think of situations we've side-stepped because they scare us, and if the symptoms of excess stress and panic are as horrible as the ones we touched upon in Chapter 1, is it any wonder?

The trouble is that in the long run this doesn't help, and **by avoiding people or places we're frightened of, our worlds can end up smaller and our lives less rewarding.**

Overcoming fear

Let me be clear, the reason I'm pausing to examine this here is not to spoil your fun – quite the opposite: I want you to experience *more* enjoyment. And when I feel worried about undertaking something new or that scares me (or both), I've found I'm far more motivated to face my fears *if I can do it in the context of something I really want to do.* And make no mistake, searching for pebbles which are perfect to paint *is* pleasurable. OK, it may not seem pleasurable if leaving the house frightens you, but if I compare it to, say, going to the dentist, I think you'll get my drift.

To take this analogy one step further, supposing as you walk to the dentist, you feel anxiety rising, begin to panic, and rush back to the house. What happens is that your immediate anxiety will decrease, but also **the message that avoidance helps to calm you starts to get hardwired into the brain.** So the next time you have to go out you feel even more filled with trepidation and soon you're panicking every time you head down the path, even if it's to go somewhere that is meant to be pleasurable, like a local stream, pond or beach to look for pebbles.

In this way anxiety begets anxiety, and we can end up being triggered by all sorts of events and situations which shouldn't necessarily make us so worried. The interesting thing is that if we ask ourselves what would happen if we remained in the situation we're avoiding, whilst we're convinced we'd pass out, throw up, collapse, have a heart attack or some such, **actually, after a certain time, what really happens is that anxiety begins to decrease of its own accord.** Those who've read the first *Making Friends with Anxiety* book or *Making Friends with Anxiety: A Calming Colouring Book* may recall this, but I wanted to mention it again as it's so important: **if we allow ourselves to ride it, eventually this anxiety passes, along with adrenaline.** But we never get to learn this if we never face it. This is why it's vital to 'feel the fear and do it anyway', as the famous author Susan Jeffers said, as then we show ourselves we can manage the situation.

TIP: 'My way of overcoming anxiety is to sit with it, instead of trying to push it away, and remind myself that I've been here before and I'm much stronger than I think. These days, I actually say to myself, "bring it on!" when I feel anxious, because nothing scares me in the way it used to.' **Tracey**

Step by step

In some respects anxiety is a 'habit' your body and mind gets into. The aim is to break that habit, as that's the key to feeling much better. But **breaking the habit of anxiety isn't something that can be done overnight or in defiance**. If you hate leaving the house and you challenge yourself to go to a party with 200 guests the first time you venture forth, you're likely to be in a state of even greater stress than usual and are more likely to beat a hasty retreat.

- **Start small and take it slow**. Begin with the easiest situation and practise it. If it's leaving the house, begin by going as far as the nearest lamppost. If it's socialising in large groups, start by meeting a friend for coffee.
- **Build up gradually** – if something is too hard, look at breaking it down into smaller, more manageable chunks. If going out for coffee scares you, invite a trusted friend round to your home where you'll feel more at ease.
- **Reward your achievements** – pat yourself on the back for each small step you take.
- **Don't focus on how far you've got to go** or berate yourself for not being able to face a huge gathering of strangers at once.
- **Stop before you have reached your ultimate goal.**
- Repeat regularly, once a day if possible, each time encouraging yourself to go a little further out of your comfort zone.
- Above all, **don't be impatient with yourself.**

TIP: 'I've learned that it's OK to ask for help. I made a pact with myself to be honest with at least one person, instead of pretending to be OK all of the time. Accepting that it's OK to not be OK has been a big learning curve for me, and knowing that I have a support system when I'm struggling has helped me feel much better.' **Andrew**

Of course your anxiety may not be that severe, and you may feel none of this is relevant to you. In which case I hope you'll forgive the detour. Now we're ready to crack on with the task in hand and put paint to pebble.

Getting started

How to paint a pebble

Pebble painting is a particularly good activity to do with children, either outside or indoors.

You will need

- **Pebbles.** Smooth, rounded stones make the best surface, so those worn by water are ideal. River stones are best, or stones found on the beach. If

45

you have a certain design in mind, such as a cat, an owl, or a caterpillar, look out for the right shape stone to be your canvas, although if you're picking up your stones from Mother Nature, please be certain you're allowed to take them. If you live nowhere near a source of stones, you can purchase bags of pebbles. Many craft shops offer a choice of small or large and light or dark so you can take your pick

- Your paint needs to be waterproof and weather proof. You can either use a mixture of two parts acrylic paint to one part PVA glue, or a chalk-based paint followed by clear varnish.

Instructions

- **Clean your stone**. If you picked up your canvas from the outdoors, you'll want to make sure it's nice and clean. Wash it with warm water and soap and pat it dry. You could even scrub it with an old toothbrush. Some stones have rough patches on them that will make painting a little more difficult. You can sand the pebble with sandpaper, starting with a coarse paper and moving to fine one until the rough patch is gone.
- **Draw your design.** It might be good to try out your design on a piece of paper beforehand. When you put it onto the rock, use a pencil or chalk. Be sure not to draw it in too heavily since it can show through the paint. Here are some design ideas you might find inspiring:

- **Now you're ready to start painting.** Be patient and move from the biggest parts of the design to the smallest, letting each coat dry before moving on. You can use a hairdryer to dry the paint faster.
- Once you've finished painting your design, **it's time to seal it**. Use a sealer and add a coat or two to make sure your art lasts for a long time.

Ways to use your finished stones

Painted pebbles have many uses. You could:

- Make them into fridge magnets – just make sure to use a light pebble and glue a magnet on the back when you're finished
- Make paperweights – heavier stones are better for this purpose
- Decorate your garden
- Create seasonal decorations
- Write inspiring messages on them

Decorated stones make great gifts and most people – unless they're very grumpy and ungracious – love to receive them. Plus you can take your inspiration from anywhere.

Chapter 5. Collage – the joy of letting rip

What is collage?

A collage is a piece of art made by sticking various different materials, such as photographs and pieces of paper or fabric, onto a backing. The word 'collage' comes from the French word 'coller', meaning 'to glue'. Like colouring, creating a collage might be something you've not done since you were a child, and whilst it can offer similar mental health benefits – helping us focus on the moment and relinquish the need to be perfect, for instance – it works on the psyche in other ways too.

Collage is free and fun

If you feel intimidated by paints, pencils and pens, you might find collage a more forgiving medium because **it allows you to change your mind before committing to your composition.** You can play around with placement and add and subtract elements until it feels right.

Conversely, if the prospect of colouring or painting pebbles seems constraining, collage is much freer and more intuitive. **It invites us to be big and bold, and offers the opportunity to make a mess, creating order from chaos.** It's also 'free' in the financial sense – the only element that you might need to purchase is glue, so if you're committed to recycling, you're onto a winner.

Almost anything can be used

By definition, a collage is made up of several different elements. Those elements can be pretty much anything, as long as you can stick it to another surface: paper, yarn, fabric, stamps, newspaper and magazine cut-outs, wallpaper, photographs, foil, labels, lids, matchsticks, corks, bark, leaves, seeds, eggshells, seashells, twigs, buttons, and so forth. You can either choose one medium (as in the collage above which I made as a

50

child, from paper), or you can use a mix, such as fabric, buttons and foil. With collage, **collecting is half the fun** – you could even go foraging in the great outdoors.

I think it's fair to describe the photograph below as a collage, although I didn't stick any of the elements down. First I gathered everything in basket (autumn leaves, a hydrangea bloom, one of my mother's sketches, a few items I use for sewing, a couple of coloured pencils and one of the teacups I was given by the photographer who shot the jacket of *One Moment, One Morning*). Then I arranged them on a plain white tablecloth, lit them as brightly as I could, and stood on a chair to photograph them from above, taking care not to fall and break my neck. I had great fun, and it's a bit of a cliché, but the only limit was my imagination.

'I love being able to imagine something, collect the materials and slowly and deliberately make it appear before my eyes.' **Cath**

Collage can bring together words and pictures

One of great aspects of collage is **that it allows us to put pictures and words together.** Ever since I used to write and illustrate my own books as a girl, I've found the way they can work in tandem fascinating. Take this example, by Debi Wilson, an administrator of the *Making Friends with Anxiety* (MFWA) Facebook group, which she put together for us:

The image of a tree makes sense without the words, and vice

versa, but the sum of both is greater than the individual parts, communicating the organic nature of the group, our connectedness, that we are continually growing and some of the topics we talk about. Many advertisements (or the wittier ones anyway) use a similar technique to be more persuasive. Likewise children's books – the best use pictures to add to the story, not just echo what the author has written.

Moreover, whilst working with words usually involves being more analytical and logical, when we're invited to marry up words with an image – or images – we can often find ourselves becoming more intuitive. **Taking time away from being rational can be a relief**, especially if we spend a lot of our work lives being that way. Debi's story is a case in point: 'I made my first picture for my sister's birthday while off sick from work with panic attacks, then my niece wanted one, then my nephew's girlfriend. I started a Facebook page called **www.facebook.com/wizzywordz** and it grew fast. Soon it was big enough for me to quit my stressful job at the council and start my own business working from home at my own pace. I love what I do now – there's nothing nicer than knowing my work can make people happy.'

<u>Getting started</u>

Make a collage using a quote you like

Why not take some words of wisdom and turn them into something visually inspiring? Here are a few suggestions:

'Some of us think holding on makes us strong; but sometimes it is letting go.' **Hermann Hesse**

'Our anxiety does not come from thinking about the future, but from wanting to control it.' **Kahlil Gibran**

'Nothing is permanent in this wicked world – not even our troubles.'
Charlie Chaplin

'The best use of imagination is creativity. The worst use of imagination is anxiety.'
Deepak Chopra

'Broken crayons still colour.' **Anon**

If none of these resonate, there are plenty of quotes to be found online. Or if the muse strikes, write your own.

Instructions

- **Once you have found a quote,** take a few minutes to **sit quietly and discover what feelings and images emerge** when you consider the words.

- **Collect** the bits and pieces that illustrate your quote in a box or basket.
- *Pinterest* is a great place to look for inspiration if you're into arts and crafts, so if you don't know the website, I strongly recommend using its facilities. If you search under 'collage' you will find numerous pinboards related to the craft.
- **Narrow down your selection** to a few elements that truly capture the essence of your quotation.
- **Choose a suitable backing**. While paper or cardboard is the usual choice, it could be wood, plastic or fabric. If items can be stuck to your surface and it's relatively flat, you can use it for making a collage.
- **Play**! Remember that you don't need to illustrate your quote literally; you can choose to tackle it in an abstract manner. Instead of using pictures of people, places or things, you might try to capture the feeling of the quote through colour, texture or simply random patterns and shapes that appeal to you. That way you'll end up with a picture that's worth a thousand words – to you, at any rate.

You might like to frame your collage so it acts as a reminder to think positively. But above all remember: there is no right or wrong way to do this, and **the journey is of value in itself**.

TIP: 'Allowing yourself to feel the way you feel stops the battle which makes the anxiety worse.' **Karen**

Keep a collage journal

If you find that you enjoy collage, you might like to keep a collage journal – a personal scrapbook filled with things you like on an ongoing basis. It could contain:

- Memories from a holiday
- Ideas for things to do
- Snippets of your children's lives – photos of them, their drawings and so on
- Tear-sheets from magazines of recipes or places you'd like to visit
- Pressed flowers and leaves
- Concert or theatre tickets
- Your favourite mantras

…or all of these. Again, search *Pinterest* under 'scrapbooking' and you'll find all sorts of clever suggestions. The great thing about having things you love all together is if you are feeling blue or wobbly, you'll have a book of happy memories and ideas to look though and to inspire you.

Chapter 6. Needlework – 'active' meditation made easy

Just as painting and putting pen to paper have been with us for centuries, so has needlecraft. Samples of Greek tapestry have been found dating from the 3rd century BC and the Victoria and Albert museum has a pair of Egyptian socks dating from the 3rd-5th century. Stitching thus **offers us a way of connecting to our ancient forbears.**

'Every time I go to sleep beneath the patchwork quilt stitched by my grandmother, it's as if I can feel her spirt envelop me, even though she's long gone.' **Sally**

Busy hands, healthy mind

What's also interesting is that occupational therapies have been used in the treatment of mental illness for a long while. Here in the UK, work in the needleroom, laundry and kitchen was prescribed to the able-bodied female patients of Bethlem

(Bedlam) lunatic asylum in the nineteenth century, for instance. And it isn't only women who were encouraged to sew: soldiers returning from WW1 were taught to stitch as active therapy for what was then called 'shell shock' – psychological breakdown caused by the trauma of trench warfare.

Back then neuroscience was still in its infancy, yet scientists have now demonstrated that many forms of needlework have a tangibly calming effect on the brain. Tapestry, for example, also stimulates brain areas related to motor skills, and entails filling in gaps with colour – it's virtually colouring-in with thread. Embroidery, patchwork, knitting, crochet – all these involve playing with pattern and making creative choices with colour.

Meditation made easy

Not only does concentrating in this way replace negative thoughts with positive ones (you're making something – woo!), it's a form of active meditation. By focusing the mind on simple tasks that require repetitive motion, it creates a sense of peace, and many people who have a difficult time with concentrative meditation (that'll be me then) can find these activities easier.

TIP: 'Make time to look after yourself – self-care is compulsory, not optional. By "self-care" I mean anything that you want to do, rather than all the stuff you think you **have** *to do. Self- care is different for each of us.'* **Alistair**

A balanced approach

All **these pastimes activate different areas of our two cerebral hemispheres, commonly known as the left and right brain.** The actions involve logic (left brain activity) as we use this to decide how to colour forms and creativity (right brain activity), which we draw upon when selecting and mixing colours. Another benefit of crafts like tapestry or patchwork, say, is their flexibility. Once we know the basics in terms of method, we can be as imaginative or guided by instructions as we wish.

<u>Getting started</u>

How to make a mobile phone case from felt

This quick project creates a case to protect your mobile phone. If you're a complete novice, for more details on techniques such as blanket stitch, visit Wikihow or YouTube.

You will need

- Felt in the colour of your choice for the base
- More felt in the colour of your choice for the embellishments
- Some buttons, perhaps, for embellishments
- Thread in a contrasting colour
- Sharp scissors
- A tapestry needle

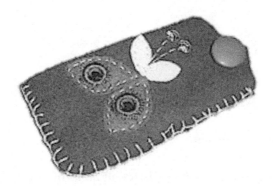

Instructions

- Measure your mobile – add a margin of about 1cm all round and cut two rectangles of felt in this size.
- Cut some shapes – leaves, flowers etc.

- Play around with your shapes on one of the rectangles (this is going to be the front) and when you are happy with your design, stitch them into place.
- Add your embellishments
- Blanket stitch about 0.5cm in around the outside edges (obviously not the top bit).

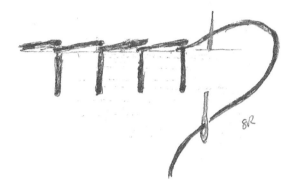

Ta-dah! You're done. Easy, wasn't it?

TIP: 'When I feel anxiety rising, I try and distract myself with a craft that I enjoy. It's all very well saying "sit with it" but I manage better when my hands are busy.' **Polly**

Chapter 7. Whittling – honing objects to use every day

If you enjoy making things, then your home may well boast several handmade items. I've made umpteen cushion covers for instance (see page 57 for a large, patchwork example) and although my husband would argue we have far more pillows, bolsters and beanbags than we could *ever* need, I believe he would concede that the pads I made to fit our garden chairs do make them a great deal more comfortable. Nonetheless, I can understand that sewing covers for cushions and cases for mobile phones is not everyone's bag. Perhaps you'd like to have a stab at something more down to earth – whittling, perhaps.

What is whittling?

Whittling is a form of wood carving where the knife strokes are clearly visible on the final piece giving it a rugged, natural feel. **The aim is to produce a stand-alone item rather than add detail to items such as furniture, and there's no limit to the range of objects you can carve**, from functional pieces like spoons, salad servers, butter spreaders, cups, ladles – even walking sticks and axes – to sculptural works of art.

'It's much more therapeutic to sit by the fire and whittle something than veg out in front of the telly,' says regular woodworker, Ben. 'Your hands know they've done something and to turn a piece of wood into a functioning tool is really satisfying. We use the bowls and spoons I've made every day at breakfast.'

Whilst carving isn't quite the new colouring and we're yet to see *The Little Book of Whittling* by Chris Lubkemann on sale at supermarket checkouts, the popularity of working with wood is growing. This is largely thanks to the internet, which enables enthusiasts across the globe to find each other and communicate instantly about their projects and ideas. Last year saw several hundred of them meet at 'Spoonfest', the first ever spoon-carving festival.

Getting started

How to carve a spoon

One of reasons whittling is so appealing is that it requires minimal outlay. Wood, a knife, a sharpener and a glove is all you need to begin.

You will need

- **Wood.** You can go scavenging for wood – with the landowner's permission – or purchase what you need from a wood supplier or carving supply shop. If you're a beginner, you're best to start off with something fairly soft and lightweight, with quite a dense grain and no knots or irregularities. Sycamore, cherry, birch, alder or hazel are all good, although the latter can be prone to splitting. Poisonous species like yew should be avoided, as should scarce or threatened woods.
- **A knife.** While traditional whittling was performed using a pocket knife, it's much easier and more comfortable to purchase a knife made specially for whittling. These generally have a fixed blade and a longer handle. Since a good beginner knife is only £10, it's a worthwhile investment.
- **A knife sharpener.** A sharpening stone is another necessity. Carving through wood is certainly going to dull the blade, and it's imperative you keep your knife sharp as you're much more likely to cut yourself with a dull knife than a sharp one.
- **A glove,** for the hand which isn't holding the knife. If you have leather work gloves one of these will do, though it may feel a bit cumbersome. If so, you can purchase specific gloves for carving which will protect your hands whilst allowing your fingers to be more flexible.

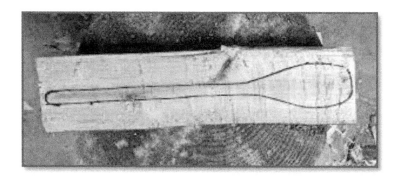

Instructions

- **Trace out your design** lightly in pencil before beginning to whittle. This will help keep you oriented as the piece begins to change and take form. Also try to work in stages, where the first stage is just getting the very basic shape, the next stage will refine closer to your final vision and continue taking light cuts off the wood until you have achieved the final shape.
- **Cut with the grain.** Carving with the grain is not only easier due to less resistance from the wood but also avoids tearing and chipping and creates a more pleasing finish. The grain is identified by the dark streaks running through the wood. You want to run the blade parallel to these streaks as opposed to cutting across the grain. Once you have identified the direction of the grain, you will need to determine which direction is with it, and which is against. The easiest way to do this is to perform a light, shallow, pushing cut away from your body in both directions – whichever offers least resistance is 'with the grain'. You should aim to make most of your cuts in this direction.

- **Types of cut.** As with any form of sculpting, there are numerous grips, cuts and leverage techniques involved in whittling. Cutting techniques include an apple-peeling motion, a pulling apart action, and a carrot-peeling method. There are YouTube videos which show the motions better than is possible on the flat page, so I recommend taking a look.
- **Drying out.** When the process is complete, your whittled object must be kept indoors for a week or so to allow the sap to dry out. Then you can sand it for a smoother finish if you wish, and to seal it, cover it in several coats of nut or sunflower oil. It can then safely be used with food, although it must be washed by hand.

If you find your initial efforts are a bit clunky-looking and uneven, that's fine. Whatever the result, **spending a few hours on this slow, traditional art is a great antidote to the stresses and strains of modern life**. Whittling is not something to be taken at a fast pace so don't rush as then you're likely to ruin your piece or cut yourself – or both. Instead relax and take it a little at a time. If you can avoid getting frustrated, you're far more likely to come away from the experience wanting to set your hands to it again.

Chapter 8. Container gardening – at one with Mother Nature

I'll come clean: when it comes to gardening, I don't plan much at all. I like to surround myself with beautiful plants, so I'll buy flowers if I like the colour. I don't care much if the instructions declare they are suited to sunshine or shade, or the soil in our tiny patio. My choices are governed by instinct, which, thinking about it in the cool light of today, is probably why only about half of what I purchase survives.

My mother, on the other hand, is more disciplined: her garden has structure. Certain plants are vetoed because the style of the foliage or horticultural heritage is found wanting. How neatly we illustrate two different approaches: I'm a 'seat-of-the-pantster'; she's a planner. And this is one of the very best things about gardening – **it accommodates all sorts of people and all levels of experience.**

Any approach is fine in my book (which this is, after all) as long as you *Do What Makes You Happy*. And **gardening can make us happy, as many a horticulturalist will testify**, and in Chapter 9 we'll explore this in more depth, but first let's try a little container gardening.

The title of this book promises activities 'anyone can do', and **the great thing about growing things in pots is that it doesn't matter if your outside space is limited**. A hanging basket or window box will add a touch of colour to your home and can help lift the spirits whenever you look at it, and it will give your neighbours and passers-by pleasure too.

Getting started

Despite the healing power of nature, the world of plants can seem intimidating to an outsider. If you're new to gardening, it's common to feel anxious you won't have green fingers, but growing flowers can be easy if you start small and take it slow. It will help to build your confidence and plants will benefit from your time and trouble.

How to plant a window box

Instructions

- **You might like to select a style of window box that matches your home** but there are no set rules: plastic, metal, terracotta, or concrete, treated softwood or hardwood – the choice is yours. Or, if you're strapped for cash, why not recycle an old container like an ice cream carton? Make sure you make drainage holes before you plant or you'll end up with water logged soil.
- **Pay attention to size.** A window box looks best if its length is within a couple of inches of the size of the window. Plants need room to grow and soil that doesn't dry out too fast – if possible, your container should be at least 8″/20cm wide to provide room for top growth and 8″/20cm deep for the roots.
- **Choose your position.** If you've a choice, a sunny exposure will please the most plants, but be warned that it will increase the amount of watering required. Don't worry too much if the only space you have available is shady – there are many excellent plants that thrive with only partial sun. Remember that some window ledges are overhung by roofing and may thus be protected from rain, in which case you'll need to check regularly for dryness. If you have a window that opens outward or a very small ledge, you will

have to secure your box beneath. **Always mount the box before you plant.**

- Use steel brackets and fasten them to the masonry with the proper screws. Rest the box on the supports and screw the bottom to the brackets.
- When it comes to growing success, **picking the right plants is key**. If your container is big enough and your budget will stretch to it, you might like to try a mix of trailing and upright plants, filler plants and bulbs. Make sure your upright plants are tall enough to be seen without blocking the window. Look for annuals such as:

- **Lobelia:** a popular choice for containers with clouds of cascading color in white, sky blue, dark blue, rose, lavender or cobalt.

- **Pansies:** perfect in any box, pansies offer prolific and long-lasting colour and are ideal for filling gaps between permanent plants or other annuals.

70

- **Petunias:** try cascading varieties as well as multi-floras for an abundance of blooms in a wide range of colours.
- **Impatiens** (also called Busy Lizzie) is *the* flowering bedding plant for shade and comes in hot pink, orange, red, white and pale pastels. New Guinea hybrids offer excellent foliage.
- **Ivy geranium** has wonderful trailing stems and bright flowers. In warmer climes it will last through winter and so is worth the initial outlay. The same is true of **geraniums**, a classic window box choice. Both can survive dry conditions fairly well, should watering not be your strong suit.
- **Ground ivy** can survive through winter in milder climates, and comes in shades of green, including variegated. Its long stems of foliage should prevent your window box from looking too sad once your annuals have died back.

- For a dramatic display, **choose plants that contrast with your container.** Bright plants can look striking against pale wood; the same is true of pale flowers against dark brick walls. Cover the drainage holes with bits of broken crockery or stones, fill with soil mixture, and firm soil around plants, leaving at least 1" at the top for watering.
- Take good care of the plants in your box, ensuring they are regularly **watered and fed** with liquid fertilizer in the growing season. Dead-head every few days to remove faded flowers, and you'll be rewarded with months of visual pleasure.

Whilst planting up a window box will probably cost you more than some of the other creative activities we've looked at thus far, **gardening is a lot more affordable than**

71

many forms of therapy. The simple act of embedding flowers in a window box can help calm and ground us. As you arrange your container, take a few moments to focus on your senses – the touch and smell of the leaves and flowers as well as how they appear. Freud said, 'Flowers are restful to look at. They have no emotions or conflict' and certainly they won't argue with you or answer back.

Tending to plants allows us to tap into the carefree part of ourselves with no deadlines, mortgage or annoying colleagues to worry about. So why not make an appointment with Mother Nature today?

Chapter 9. Sowing seeds – growing yourself better

I remember when my mother first gave me a little spot in our garden to tend; I must have been about five. I demarcated it with stones and planted forget-me-nots and poached eggs (Limnanthes douglasii) – flowers that still make me smile. Having to care for plants is a good way to learn responsibility for other living things and when we are small it helps us to develop an appreciation of the magic of nature. The same is true for us as adults too. On one level, it means we can surround ourselves with plants we like aesthetically, but it goes deeper than that.

Why is gardening such good therapy?

- **Gardening connects us to something ancient and primal.** Our forebears have been demarcating plots and tilling the land for millennia.

- **It allows us all to be nurturers**. Horticulture is a great equalizer: it doesn't matter if we are seven or seventy, rich or poor, plants don't give a fig who is tending them, and it can boost self-esteem to be involved in such a transformative activity.
- **Cultivating other living things takes us out of ourselves**. Self-absorption can contribute to anxiety and stress and focusing on the great outdoors – even in the pared-down form of a patio or roof terrace – encourages us to be less insular. Gardening serves to remind us that we are not the centre of the universe.
- **Gardening allows us to feel safe**. To dig and delve in a walled or fenced garden also helps to contain us within boundaries both literally and metaphorically, allowing us to feel safe at the same time as expanding our horizons.
- **Being amongst plants and flowers reminds us to live in the present moment**. We saw in Chapter 1 that anxiety tends to lessen when we let go of ruminating on the past or worrying about the future. Like many of the activities described so far, gardening allows us to become more present.
- **Gardening engages all the senses.** Next time you're in a garden, pause for a few moments and allow yourself to be aware of what's around you. Experiencing the fullness of nature can be very restorative.

TIP: 'Mindfulness has really helped me. When I feel bad, I don't struggle against my emotions, I observe them and breathe. I try to see them as temporary feelings – like clouds floating through the sky. I'll name the emotions "anger" or "anxiety" or whatever, say" hi" and let them go.' **Philip**

TIP: 'I take 5 or 10 minutes to appreciate something lovely, like a nice plant or tree with the blue (or grey!) sky in the background. It's a mindfulness tool and I find it invaluable.' **Helen**

- **Gardening helps us relax and let go.** Moreover, the rhythm of tasks like weeding, hoeing, sowing and sweeping means thoughts can ebb and flow along with our movements. I sometimes take to watering the pots on our patio when trying to untangle knots in plotting which can arise when writing novels. Often the solution comes to me far more easily outside than if I were to continue sitting staring and despairing at my screen.

- **Working in nature releases happy hormones.** To say that gardening encourages us to exercise and spend time outdoors is obvious, but it's worth reminding ourselves that what's good for the body is also good for the mind. When we exercise, levels of serotonin and dopamine (hormones that make us feel good) rise and the level of cortisol (a hormone associated with stress), is lowered. It's true that a day in the garden can leave you ready to hit the hay earlier than usual, but it can also get rid of excess energy so you sleep better and wake feeling renewed inside.

- **Gardening reminds us of the cycle of life** and thus helps us come to terms with that most universal of anxieties: death. In the plant world, regeneration is a matter of course, but psychological repair does not necessarily come so easily to us as human beings. One way of working through difficult emotions is through rituals, and gardening is a form of ritual involving both the giving of life and acknowledgement of its end. As such it works within our minds as a symbolic act: it's no coincidence that we create gardens of remembrance and mark the scattered ashes and graves of our loved ones with roses, shrubs and trees; by doing so we're acknowledging that from dust we all come and to dust we return.

- **Gardening allows us to vent anger and aggression.** Why beat pillows with a baseball bat or yell at the cat when you have a hedge to hack? There are times when I enjoy cutting and chopping, yanking and binding as much, if not more, than sowing, feeding and watering, and the great thing about destructiveness in the garden is that it can be in the service of growth – if you don't cut back plants, you'll be swamped by them.
- **Gardening can be a good way of gaining a sense of control.** When we're stressed, we often feel more easily overwhelmed, and this can perpetuate the cycle of anxiety. But whereas trying to control other people is invariably a fruitless exercise, you're more likely to succeed in controlling your hedges, beds and borders.

Getting started

How to grow summer flowers from seed

If you've got a little outside space, one of the great joys of gardening is that it allows us to enjoy quiet time, alone, with the earth in a literal sense. You don't need acres of land to enjoy the feeling of soil in your fingers; a small patch is space enough.

Instructions

I recommend looking for packets that say 'Ideal for Children' – who cares if you left school years ago? This isn't about challenging yourself to do something tricky, it's about getting pleasure from watching plants grow. For the same reason I suggest starting off with seeds that can be sown directly into the soil. That way you won't have to worry about buying trays

77

and compost, or making space to keep them indoors until they're ready to plant out. If you're an experienced gardener, doubtless you'll be familiar with these suggestions, but if you're new to working with the soil, the odds are that you will find them rewarding. They're easy to grow and relatively inexpensive, offering you more flowers for your pennies!

SR

- **Sunflower.** Just sow the seeds straight into the ground in a sunny, sheltered spot. Follow the instructions on the packet and watch them grow and grow – some varieties can reach 14′ Just be sure to provide the stems with supports.

78

- **Sweet Pea.** Who can resist their delicious fragrance? The large seeds of sweet peas are easy to handle. A sunny spot, a supportive fence and plenty of water is all these climbers need to produce home-grown cut flowers; the good news is that the more you pick, the more flowers they produce. They do well in containers as long as they have support to climb, but wherever you plant them, keep an eye out for slugs and snails as they find the young shoots very appetising.

- **Eschscholzia (Californian Poppy).** If your schedule means you might not manage regular watering, then Californian Poppies are a good bet. These colourful annuals thrive in poor, dry soil and full sun so are perfect for spots where other flowers might struggle. Scatter them where you want them to flower and let them take care of themselves, creating effortless drifts of colour.

- **Nasturtium.** Quick growing and colourful, I might have been gardening for several years, but I still swear by nasturtiums. I plant them in containers so they spill over, but you can equally well sow the seeds directly into borders as ground cover – just make sure the danger of frosts has passed. Like Californian Poppy, Nasturtium flourish in poor soil. (My next-door-neighbour has joined me in planting some on the wasteland opposite so we can see them from our bedroom windows, for instance.) The leaves are edible – they taste peppery, a bit like rocket – and the flowers too, so if you can bear to eat the attractive blooms, try them in a salad or as a pretty garnish.

TIP: *'I like to sow new seeds and watch them grow into young plants, to wander around and see what has grown in my garden overnight. To feel the earth in my hands is incredibly healing.'* **Nikki**

Chapter 10. Baking – making magic in the kitchen

When I was a teenager, my mother used to observe that she could tell when I'd had a bad day at school because I would come home and make fudge. Whilst I'm not sure this is entirely accurate (I made an awful lot of fudge, and I wasn't *that* miserable at school) nonetheless she has a point: cooking is an effective method of reducing anxiety, and if a survey of one is anything to go by, baking cakes and making sweets is particularly therapeutic. Given what we've learned thus far about the workings of the mind and body, it's easy to see why.

Baking and body consciousness

'Baking and *body consciousness*? You're having a laugh,' cynics may scoff. But bear with me: alongside the comfort that comes from eating what you've made, baking offers a good opportunity to be mindful. Just like the other activities we've looked at, **the physical acts involved in baking force you to focus on something outside your whirling thoughts and connect you to your body.** Measuring ingredients, sifting flour, beating eggs, kneading bread – all these help distract from self-reflection and worry and encourage us to focus on the present moment. And the good thing is that because **baking encourages us to slow down and focus on one task**, we don't have to force ourselves to concentrate; it tends to happen inevitably, just as it does when we're painting glass or pebbles, sewing or gardening. Or, to put it more bluntly: whipping boiling sugar into fluffy pillows requires your undivided attention because if you waver, you'll get burnt!

John Whaite, previous winner of *The Great British Bake Off*, was diagnosed with bipolar disorder 10 years ago and has spoken openly about how he finds baking therapeutic. 'When I'm in the kitchen, measuring the amount of sugar, flour or butter I need for a recipe or cracking the exact number of eggs, I am in control,' he says. 'That's really important, as a key element of my condition is a feeling of no control.'

Don't beat yourself up

A desire to feel in control is a common trait of many stressed and anxious people, but whilst it can be soothing to gain a sense of orderliness, **it's simply not possible to be in control of every aspect of our lives, and one of the benefits of baking is that it also teaches us to let go of that desire.** As author Julia

Ponsonby explains in her book, *The Art of Mindful Baking*, accepting that things will happen when they're ready is a useful life tool.

Whatever you knead

'It might seem counterintuitive, but **when my stress levels are extremely high I choose longer culinary projects,'** says Adrienne, one of the many Facebook group members who lives in the US. 'I might opt for a sourdough loaf, for instance, as the process can take up to 24 hours and you have to let the dough develop at its own pace and observe it. Plus you have to knead it by hand, which connects me to my physicality and this then helps to reduce my mental anxiety.'

Adrienne suggests taking on something swift as a shorter-term stress reliever. 'When I'm worried but not quite so hyped up, I make chocolate-chip cookies. It takes me about 25 minutes to go from a state of anxiety to the freshly-baked result. My outlook tends to be more positive when I have accomplished something and have yummy and home-made goodies to eat.'

Sweet versus savoury

One reason baking can be particularly pleasing is that **it gives you something *tangible* at the end** of your endeavors. OK, so your cake may not warrant a plinth in the Tate, but still, it is a thing: it has edges, it can be decorated, and it can be held out with pride to guests. Whereas Irish stew, or a curry, well, they're not the same. Don't get me wrong, I'm married to a chef, and I love savoury food, but the parallel to a sculptural work of art is less obvious.

Baking combines a heap of powders which have no real-world meaning (to conceptualize flour, for example, feels impossible), then adding something wet, heating it up and watching it change, writes Sophie Johnson in *The Guardian*. She believes that baking requires – and imbues – a kind of trust that is absent in everyday cooking. She uses asparagus as an example. When you coat a stalk in oil and throw it on a cast-iron skillet, the result is logical: it is still asparagus, if hotter and softer. On the other hand, the premise that flour and water and sugar and yeast – which are almost useless on their own – could combine to make something like a loaf of bread requires trust.

I agree, but I feel that baking is about more than that – it's about *magic*. That's what I liked about making cakes as a girl – the ingredients went into the oven looking flat and unappetising, and came out transformed. Like the pumpkin the fairy turned into Cindererella's coach, the frog who turned into a prince; the 'ta-dah!' of a risen cake is the abracadabra of the culinary world.

Considerations, whatever you choose to make

- **Take a moment to close your eyes** and allow yourself to envisage what you're making. If it's the crumble recipe featured on pages 84-86, picture the gloopy fruity dark base with its golden topping… Savour how it will taste – the combination of tart blackberries and cooking apples offset by the sweet crumble topping, the different textures on the tongue… That should whet the appetite.
- **Then give your kitchen a quick clean**. Cleaning (as long as it doesn't become obsessive) is a good way of reducing the physical manifestations of anxiety.
- **Pick a reliable recipe**. It's disheartening when recipes don't work, and when you are baking to reduce stress this is especially important.
- To repeat what I said earlier: *Do What Makes You Happy*. In this context this means **bake what you want**. Julia Ponsonby suggests baking 'with integrity'; using ingredients that have been grown organically and sourced locally, so you know they will be less damaging to the environment. But if you're in a state of high anxiety you may not feel in the right headspace to shop ethically. If that's you, remember that this is baking to make you feel better,

so tell that anxiety gremlin to keep schtum and get into a 'this is a treat' mentality.

- **Enlist a helper.** Invite a friend to help you bake and enjoy sharing what you've made together.

- Alternatively, you may prefer to **cook in quiet solitude**. Remember your purpose is to reduce anxiety so adopt the strategy that will help you de-stress most effectively.

- **Engage in the whole process**, whatever the outcome. So the top of your soufflé is burned? Your sponge has sagged? Remind yourself the only person who really minds is you, so try not yourself in a stress about the results being perfect every time.

'When I'm stressed, I say to myself, "Gracie, what are you getting so wound up about? You're in competition with no one but yourself. You're gonna win whatever!"' **Grace**

Getting started

How to make a blackberry and apple crumble

There are tens of thousands of recipes out there for cakes not to mention all those for different kinds of bread, sweets and biscuits, so it's hard to choose just one for this book. Much of what follows can be adapted should you choose to make something else, but I've chosen crumble for two reasons: firstly because it's a dish that even the most inexperienced cook should be able to manage, and secondly because if you choose to make one from blackberry and apple (which is my personal favourite) it provides you with a double dose of pleasure, as **alongside baking, it gives you the perfect excuse to go...**

Blackberry picking

The best time to look for blackberries is from late August, when the scent of autumn is in the air. There should be no need to venture far: head off to a riverbank, alleyway, hedgerow or park armed with a pot or two (empty ice-cream cartons are good) and pick what you need. Don't take more – there are laws governing foraging for fruit, and there may be others keen to harvest from the same patch.

- Don't pick too low down (dogs may pee there) or high up (birds may have had a good nibble)
- Avoid the side of busy roads (car exhaust, ugh)
- Wear long sleeves and trousers
- Aim to pick the plumpest berries

If you do not feel like baking your crumble at the same time as you go picking, don't worry; the fruit freezes well and can be used many weeks – even months – later. Don't wash them until you're about to eat or freeze them or the berries will go soggy.

Ingredients for the crumble (serves 4):

6oz/180g plain flour
3oz/90g caster sugar
3oz/90g butter, cut into pieces

These proportions can be altered to suit your taste. Some cooks suggest 2oz sugar, 4oz butter and 6oz of flour, but if (like me) you like your crumble wickedly buttery and sweet, you can adjust the proportion to 4oz sugar, 4oz butter and 6oz flour. If you like extra 'fluff' to your topping, try self-raising rather than plain flour, or you can swap half of your flour for grated almonds for a richer, nuttier flavour.

Ingredients for the base:

- 10oz/300g Braeburn apples
- 4oz/115g blackberries
- 1oz/30g unsalted butter

- 1oz/30g demerara sugar
- ¼ tsp ground cinnamon (if you like the taste)

Again, you can adjust these measures. You may like a thicker fruit base and less crumble, or vice versa. When you've made your crumble once, you can experiment next time.

Method

- Heat the oven to 190C/170C fan/gas mark 5.
- Tip the flour and sugar into a large bowl. Add the butter and rub into the flour using your fingertips until it is a light crumbly texture, like breadcrumbs.
- Peel, core and cut the apples into 1"/2.5cm dice.
- Put the butter and sugar into a pan and melt over a medium heat. Cook for a couple of minutes until the mixture turns to a light caramel. Stir in the apples and cook for three minutes, then add the blackberries and cinnamon.
- Remove from heat and spoon the fruit into an ovenproof dish, top with the crumble mix and heat in the oven until cooked through and golden brown on top – depending on the depth of your dish, this will be 15-25 minutes.

Serve with a dollop of vanilla ice cream, crème fraiche, cream, natural yoghurt or go the whole hog and smother in custard. Delicious!

'At the age of 24, I was hospitalized as a result of an eating disorder. Once a week we attended craft sessions and to engage in a creative process, use my hands and practise a mindful activity helped me to build my self-esteem. Hitherto, I'd felt so easily defeated that the small act of making a bracelet was a mighty triumph, and slowly my confidence began to grow.' **Florence**

Becoming more confident

It is not only those with addictions or eating disorders who suffer from low self-esteem. Research shows that up to 8 out of 10 women are dissatisfied with their reflection when looking in a mirror, and more than half may see a distorted body image. Men are more likely to be happy with what they see or indifferent, but we all have times when we don't feel good about ourselves.

Suffering from a deep-rooted lack of confidence over a prolonged period has a harmful effect on our mental health; we tend to see ourselves and our lives in a more negative and critical light and feel less able to rise to any

91

challenges thrown our way. We are more inclined to hide away from social situations and stop trying new things – the kind of avoidance tactics we explored in Chapter 4 – and suffer from anxiety and/or depression.

'I was always creatively inclined as a child, and loved making stuff,' says Martha Prince, who made the necklace below. 'I hadn't realised how important that was to me until I experienced my first clinical depression. Away from home, lost in an un-diagnosed fog of blue, I started self-harming. My GP noticed – probably the way I kept tugging my sleeve down – and she, bless her heart, opened her bottom drawer, and pulled out knitting needles and yarn. "Right," she said. "I teach all my girls to knit. When you feel the urge to harm – knit instead. Give yourself something to do with your hands, so they don't turn to hurting you." I became very proficient in squares, but knitting did not float my boat. The big wall of beads in the craft shop did though... I'd go in to buy wool, and find myself staring at the beads for half an hour, an hour, seeing possibilities whizzing through my mind. I finally bit the bead, and bought some, and have never looked back.'

The drive to build self-esteem isn't about vanity therefore, nor is it a pie-in-the-sky ambition; **if we're looking to reduce depression, manage our levels of anxiety and stress and improve our sense of wellbeing, it's important to develop new and positive ways of seeing ourselves**. Even if low confidence is the result of what happened when you were growing up, that doesn't mean you have to be stuck with it forever. Clearly this isn't the place to psychoanalyse your past – you'll need to see a specialist for that, and if you're interested, visit *The British Association for Counselling and Psychotherapy* (www.bacp.co.uk) to find a registered therapist near you. But there are a few ways you can help improve how you feel about yourself if you are keen to be more confident.

JK

93

- **Recognise what you're good at.** Rather than focusing on the mistakes you might have made, consider your achievements and what you enjoyed, and build on those successes. Take the activities in this ebook: if you've tried one or two, notice if your default is to dismiss your creations and make a concerted effort not to. It might sound hackneyed, but **being kind to yourself is key**.

- **Start saying 'no'.** People with low self-esteem often feel they have to say 'yes' to other people's requests even when they don't really want to. It's easy to see why this might exacerbate anxiety and stress, so try to be less agreeable! If you find saying 'no' hard, start by saying 'I'll come back to you' or 'let me think about it'. This gives you the chance to give pause to consider if you *really* want to do what is being asked of you.

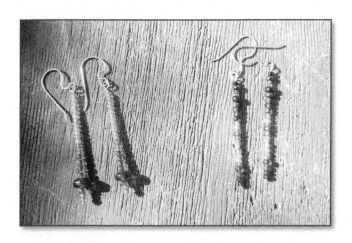

- **Give yourself a challenge**. We all feel nervous or afraid at times – I've been banging on about how 'normal' this is since Chapter 1 – but **letting our**

94

nerves get the better of us perpetuates the cycle of low self-esteem. Setting yourself a goal is a good way to boost confidence, as if you achieve it you'll feel good about yourself. And remember, those challenges don't have to be huge, or done in one hit. Break them down into manageable steps and pat yourself on the back as you go.

Creating something precious

Like colouring or collage, a handmade item of jewellery is a form of self-expression. As with so many crafts, the process of designing and making your item can give you a lift. In addition, a handmade necklace, bracelet or earrings can help us feel more individually attractive and special. By creating something to wear ourselves (like Martha's earrings here), we are saying that *we* are worth looking at.

95

- **You don't have to use things that are ready-made.** Jewellery-making gives you lots of opportunities to include your own components. You could work in trinkets with personal significance – a hand-me-down locket, a family heirloom or a single earring, maybe. You could use your own handmade beads. Hell, you could even whittle some from wood!
- **Making jewellery can be as simple or challenging as you wish.** It's possible to produce something very beautiful with nothing more complicated than beads and thread. But there are all sorts of skills you can learn, so every time you sit down at a table to make something, it can be as fresh and exciting as the very first time you picked up a pair of pliers.
- **Making jewellery doesn't have to be all about you.** It can also be very rewarding to create a personalized piece for someone you know and love. When Martha made the headdress (shown on the previous page) for my wedding day and gave it to me as a surprise I was especially delighted because she had *made* it.

Getting started

How to make an endless beaded necklace

If you make a necklace that is long enough to go over your head, there is no need to add a clasp. This has several advantages. Firstly, there's no need to fiddle doing it up. Secondly, it'll save you having to buy a clasp and attach it. And thirdly, if you're allergic to metal, it means your necklace won't trigger a reaction.

You will need

- Beading thread
- Super glue or clear nail varnish
- Beads of your choice (e.g., glass, stone, ceramic, precious or base metal, etc.)
- Salvaged trinkets
- Strong beading needles
- Tape measure
- Scissors

TIP: 'With a beading needle, stiffness is less important than having a slim "eye" that will fit through your beads. One of my favourite beading needles is a piece of doubled over and twisted fuse wire.'
Martha

Instructions

- **Choose a quiet and comfortable place** where you can concentrate without many interruptions. Make sure to have all of your materials ready.
- **Determine the length of your necklace.** When considering which style of necklace you'd like to create, remember that it needs to be long enough to go over your head (approximately 26"/66cms or more). Take your tape measure, and loop it around your neck while looking at yourself in the mirror. You might want your necklace to wrap around your neck a few times, or be just one long loop. Experiment to see which you prefer.
- **Arrange your beads and trinkets on a flat surface such as a tray or table.** You will find it easier to have

a piece of soft cloth under them – they will bounce less if you drop them, and if you roll the edges up they are less likely to roll off or away.

- Try different colour variations of beads and using a central piece or pieces. **Play around until you find the design you like best.**

- Once you're satisfied with your design, **make a looped knot in one end of your thread** to ensure that the beads stay on.

- **Carefully remove one bead at a time, and string it onto the thread.** Be sure to leave about 3-4"/7.5-10cm/ of stringing material at the end.

- **Be careful not to pull the thread too tight.** Leave a small amount of slack in the necklace (¼"/2-4mm). This will allow the beads to move and rotate, so they don't rub on each other or the thread too much. If the stringing material is too tight the necklace will be rigid and this can make the design look angular rather than rounded.

- **To finish, knot the end of the thread together with the loop of thread you made in the beginning.** Trim the excess thread and add a bit of glue to reinforce the knot.

Wear your necklace with pride and enjoy!

'When I'm struggling – can't get out of bed because the world doesn't feel safe enough – I know I can open my bead box, choose colours that call to me, and create something beautiful. Something that involves problem solving: "Now, how am I going to get the beads to hang like that...?" and the triumph of having worked it out: "AH! Yes! Knot it there!" Because I love seed beads, it also takes concentration, and dexterity. And patience: "This needle is too big for this bead. Let's find another bead... Or perhaps another needle..." I get completely lost in the here and now of turning an idea into reality, and the anxiety/depression melts into the background,' says Martha.

'At the end I have a beautiful thing that I created. I may not have left the bed all day, but I can hold onto the fact that I have made something new. And then there's the affirming glory of wearing it out and people commenting, "Oh, that's lovely, where did you get it?" and I get to say, "Thank you. I made it." I always try to breathe that compliment in. I made something that other people think is beautiful: **Inhale**. And then I follow it up with I made something that I think is beautiful: **Inhale**.'

Chapter 12. Looking and listening

By now I hope you're seeing a pattern. Whilst colouring might be the de-stressing activity 'du jour', there are many other creative pursuits that work on the mind in a similar fashion and can also lessen the grip that anxiety holds on us. My own 'arts and crafts therapies' include drawing, taking photographs, gardening and sewing as they feel so different from my day job of writing. My husband, Tom, expresses his creativity by cooking (that's him on page 80).

Keeping the creative juices flowing

Of course the more we each engage in an activity, the more accomplished we tend to become, but I've already mentioned that we anxious types are prone to perfectionism anyway, and can all too easily berate ourselves for not being as brilliant as we want to be. Again, tell your anxiety gremlin to 'shush!' then you can get on with 'being' a colourist/photographer/ gardener/ cook or painter rather than 'doing' it. **'Doing' tends to feel like a duty and focuses on the end result; 'being' is about living in the present moment.**

Yet no matter how much we might enjoy the feeling of accomplishment that we get when we complete a project or create something beautiful, it's not always easy to motivate ourselves. **When we're feeling weary or depressed, it's more difficult to engage in the 'work' part of the work-and-reward cycle our brains need to thrive.** Plus, however hard I try to lure you into various activities, I imagine one or two of you are still saying: 'It's no good! I'm just not creative.' Whilst I beg to differ – just as everyone is anxious, *everyone* is creative – nonetheless I appreciate that taking up a creative pursuit isn't for everyone and sometimes the time isn't right. The last thing I want is to add another guilt-inducing obligation to your 'to do' list. That would only make your worry worse – the very opposite of what this little book aims to do – which is why, in this last chapter, we're going to investigate how we can connect to creativity even when we don't feel like making anything ourselves.

TIP: *'Realise that some days it's OK to do nothing and achieve nothing. Because YOU are important.'* **Ali**

The healing powers of art

As brothers Jeff and Allan Rogers observe on their blog *The Psychology of Beauty*, knowing how to stimulate feelings of reward and pleasure during our low periods is key to emerging from them as quickly as possible, and thanks to a new study by researchers at the Emory University School of Medicine, we now know there's an easy way to accomplish this: simply *look at art*.

The Emory study revealed that there is something special about viewing art; it more strongly activates the brain's 'reward system' than other forms of pleasurable visual stimulation. When the researchers analysed the brain activity of the study participants while viewing the works of Monet, Van Gogh, Picasso and others, versus viewing plain photographic images of similar subjects, they found that the brain's ventral striatum (a part of the reward system) was more active while viewing the works of art.

Whether the participants actually *liked* what they saw didn't matter. The study subjects simply viewed both paintings and photographs whilst researchers scanned their brains using functional magnetic resonance imaging (fMRI), taking note of the various areas of activity. This unbiased assessment revealed that the regions which were stimulated by art images rather than photographs operated independently of those areas in the brain which were stimulated by aesthetic preference. In addition to the ventral striatum, viewing art stimulated the hypothalamus and the orbito-frontal cortex; looking at the photographic images did not have the same impact. According to research associate Simon Lacey, Ph.D., 'The brain's responses to art may have a connection to the reward circuit and perceptions of luxury or social status, independent of whether an individual rates the image in question highly.' According to their theory, **just looking at paintings or sculpture should be stimulating, even if you don't find the pieces particularly pleasing to look at.** If you're interested, you can find the full results of the Emory study online in the journal *NeuroImage*.

Other studies have made similar findings. Professor Semir Zeki has shown that looking at art releases that neurotransmitter dopamine into the orbito-frontal cortex of the brain, resulting in feelings of intense pleasure similar to being in love.

You might like to put the researchers' hypotheses to the test and head off to an art gallery. Who knows? Perhaps a trip to the look at paintings could do more for your sense of wellbeing than going on a date!

Listening to music can alleviate anxiety

Joking aside, it's not always easy to find time to look at art. Maybe you're nowhere near a gallery or you're simply too busy or tired to go anywhere, but **there *is* a way you can gain the therapeutic benefit of creativity from the comfort of your armchair: by listening to music.**

- **Music can have a beneficial effect on our physiological functions**, slowing the pulse and heart rate, lowering blood pressure and decreasing the levels of stress hormones.
- **Music can be a great aid to meditation**, helping to prevent the mind wandering.
- **Calming music before bedtime promotes peace and relaxation** and helps to induce sleep.

'I'm a teacher and I often listen to music whilst doing my admin/session-prepping. It can be classical or pop – the main thing is to choose something uplifting. This has a knock-on effect when it comes to my lessons, as it puts me in a relaxed state of mind and means I approach them with a happy heart.' **Helen**

I'm sure you don't need me to tell you that if you're stuck in a traffic jam or waiting for an appointment, tuning into a favourite song can reduce the stress you're under. But sometimes, if we're anxious, we can avoid creating the space to listen music. Perhaps it feels like a waste of time, not helping to achieve anything. Obviously musical preferences vary widely and you know what you like, but if you've not tried it before, you may find slow, gentle classical music is most effective when you're worried.

JK

TIP: 'When it comes to quietening the mind, I find instrumental music more soothing than anything with vocals. It's as if my head is full enough with all my whirling thoughts, and I can't take in any more. Whereas if I play a Beethoven piano sonata or one of Bach's violin concertos, then I can feel my whole body relax.' **Lesley**

106

If you find it hard to **incorporate music into a busy schedule**, try listening to CDs or downloads in the car, or turning the radio on when in the bath or shower. Take portable music with you when walking the dog, or put the stereo on instead of the TV. And it doesn't always have to be something low key and soothing – **singing (or shouting) along can be a great release of tension** too. Productivity increases when stress is reduced, so it's likely to be worthwhile in the long run. Like all the activities in this little book, it just takes a small effort to begin with.

A note about photography

Initials JK © johnknightphotography.co.uk, CN © Catherine Newell, MP © Martha Prince, DW ©Debi Wilson and image on p45 with kind permission from stores.ebay.co.uk/alienstoatdesigns/

Images on p14, 18, 20, 21, 23, 24, 26, 28, 31, 32, 34, 35, 56, 60, 62, 63, 68, 70, 75,80,82, 91, 97 101,102,103 and 105 are available free from http://pngimg.com/ or **https://pixabay.com/**

All other images, © Sarah Rayner

Thank you

I hope you've found this book enjoyable to read, and helpful too. I'd like to thank all the members of *Making Friends with Anxiety Facebook group*, especially those who contributed their illustrations, tips and insights to share with other sufferers here, and the amazing team of Admins who do their utmost to make a safe space to discuss anxiety issues. **If you'd like to join the group, our door is open to all over 16. Find us at www.facebook.com/groups/makingfriendswithanxiety/.**

SR

About Sarah Rayner

Sarah Rayner is the author of five novels including the international bestseller, *One Moment, One Morning* and the two follow-ups which also feature her Brighton-based characters, *The Two Week Wait* and *Another Night, Another Day*.

Friendship is a theme common to all Sarah's novels, and it's a thread that connects to her non-fiction titles too. In 2014 she published *Making Friends with Anxiety, a little self- help book to help ease worry and panic*. This was followed by *Making Friends with Anxiety: A Calming Colouring Book* with illustrator Jules Miller and this book, along with.*Making Friends with the Menopause* and *Making Friends with Depression* in collaboration with Dr Patrick Fitzgerald and Kate Harrison.

Sarah lives in Brighton with her husband, Tom, and stepson, Sebastian. You can find her on Facebook, on Twitter and her website is www.sarah-rayner.com

JK

NON-FICTION BY SARAH RAYNER

Making Friends with Anxiety:
A warm, supportive little book to help ease worry and panic

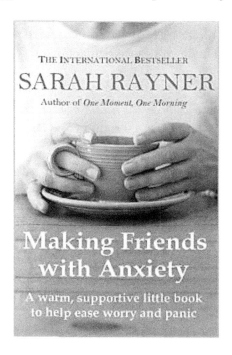

Paperback £4.99, ebook £1.99
Rated 4.7*s on Amazon

'*Simple, lucid advice on how to accept your anxiety*' **Matt Haig, bestselling author of *Reasons to Stay Alive.***

Drawing on her experience of anxiety disorder and recovery, Sarah Rayner explores this common and often distressing condition with candour and humour. She reveals the seven elements that commonly contribute to anxiety, including adrenaline, negative thinking and fear of the future, and explains why it becomes such a problem for many of us.

Packed with tips and exercises, this companion to mental good health draws on the techniques of Mindfulness-based Cognitive Therapy, yet reads like a chat with a friend. If you suffer from panic attacks, a debilitating disorder or just want to reduce the amount of time you spend worrying, this simple little book will give you a greater understanding of how your mind and body work together, helping restore confidence and control.

'Reads like chatting with an old friend; one with wit, wisdom and experience' **Laura Lockington, Brighton and Hove Independent**

'Sarah's advice is very sage: if one is prone to anxiety, as many of us are, it is futile to expect to be totally rid of it forever. It will come back, but it is possible to tame it. She encourages the reader to be kinder to themselves, live in the moment, and accept their anxiety as an occasionally troublesome, yet integral part of their own being. Deeply personal yet eminently practical, this accessible and engaging e-book should prove extremely helpful to anyone trying to cope with anxiety.' **Dr Ian Williams, GP and author**

Making Friends with Anxiety: A Calming Colouring Book
with illustrations by Jules Miller

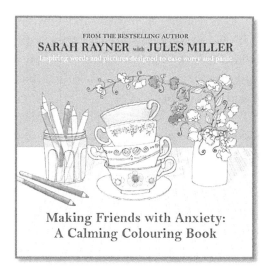

A beautiful adult colouring book packed with tips and insights to encourage mindfulness and ease worry and panic.

Out now in paperback £3.99
Rated 4.6*s on Amazon

Alongside a series of beautifully-crafted pictures, Sarah Rayner explains with warmth and humour how to 'make friends with anxiety' and thereby manage stress. She shows why some of us are prone to anxiety and why colouring, in particular, can be so therapeutic. She then explores other creative activities that can have a similar effect on the psyche, providing readers with a wide array of solutions that encourage mindfulness and help reduce worry.

This text is offset by Jules Miller's detailed illustrations designed to maximize the pleasure of zoning out from day-to-day worries and becoming absorbed in colouring. There are abstract patterns and cheery animals, gorgeous flowers and quirky landscapes, and each picture incorporates a 'mantra' – a few simple words to reflect upon and help boost your mood whenever you look at it. The result is a book to treasure – a unique combination of wit and wisdom that can encourage positivity long after the colouring is done.

Making Friends with Depression:
A warm and wise companion to recovery

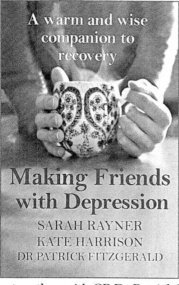

From the bestselling authors of *Making Friends with Anxiety* and *The 5/2 Diet Book* comes a clear and comforting book to help sufferers of depression.

If you're suffering from depression or low mood, you can end up feeling very alone, desperately struggling to find a way through, but recovery *is* possible and bestselling authors Sarah Rayner and Kate Harrison, together with GP Dr Patrick Fitzgerald show you how. They explain that hating or fighting the 'black dog' of depression can actually prolong your suffering, whereas 'making friends' with your darker emotions by compassionately accepting these feelings can restore health and happiness.

Sarah and Kate write with candour, compassion and humour because they've both been there and, together with Dr Patrick Fitzgerald, have produced a concise and practical guide to help lift low mood and support the journey to recovery. It explains:

* The different types of depressive illness
* Where to seek help and how to get a diagnosis
* The pros and cons of the most common medications
* The different kinds of therapy available

* Why depression can cause so many physical symptoms
* What to do if you suffer suicidal thoughts
* How to stop the spiral of negative thinking

* The link between poor self-esteem and depression
* And why hating depression can make it much worse

Fully illustrated by Sarah Rayner and reflecting the latest National Institute for Health and Care Excellence guidelines, *Making Friends with Depression* is much more than a memoir; it aims to help you see how depression can feed on itself and show you ways to break that cycle by treating your body and mind with understanding and kindness. You'll find realistic suggestions on eating and exercise, advice on self-medicating with drink and drugs, as well as tips on reaching out and avoiding relapse, all delivered with a surprising lightness of touch. The result is book that doesn't shy away from the bleakness or difficulties of the subject but remains tender and life-affirming, offering hope and guidance through the darkest of times.

Out now on Amazon: Paperback £4.99, ebook £1.99

Making Friends with the Menopause:
A clear and comforting guide to support you as your body changes

Many women consider the menopause anything but a friend, but together with Dr Patrick Fitzgerald, Sarah Rayner explains why rather than fighting or ignoring the changes our bodies go through, understanding the experience can help us feel a whole heap better.

Just why does stopping menstruating cause such profound hormonal shifts in the body, leading us to react in myriad ways physically and mentally? Here you'll find the answers, along with practical advice on hot flushes and night sweats, anxiety and mood swings, muscular aches and loss of libido, early-onset menopause, hysterectomy and more, plus a simple overview of each stage of the process so you'll know what to expect in the years before, during and after.

Paperback £6.99, ebook £1.99
Rated 4.6*s on Amazon

FICTION BY SARAH RAYNER

One Moment, One Morning

'A real page-turner . . . You'll want to inhale it in one breath' **Easy Living**

The Brighton to London line. The 07:44 train. Carriages packed with commuters. A woman applies her make-up. Another observes the people around her. A husband and wife share an affectionate gesture. Further along, a woman flicks through a glossy magazine. Then, abruptly, everything changes: a man has a heart attack, and can't be resuscitated; the train is stopped, an ambulance called. For three passengers on the 07:44, life will never be the same again...

The Two Week Wait

'Carefully crafted and empathetic' **Sunday Times**
'Explores an emotive subject with great sensitivity' **Sunday Express**

After a health scare, Brighton-based Lou learns that her time to have a baby is running out. She can't imagine a future without children, but her partner doesn't feel the same way. Meanwhile, up in Yorkshire, Cath is longing to start a family with her husband, Rich. No one would be happier to have a child than Rich, but Cath is infertile. Could these two women help each other out?

Another Night, Another Day

'An irresistible novel about friendship, family and dealing with life's blows' **Woman & Home**

Three people, each crying out for help . . . There's Karen, worried about her dying father; Abby, whose son has autism and needs constant care; and Michael, a family man on the verge of bankruptcy. As each sinks under the strain, they're brought together at Moreland's Clinic. Here, behind closed doors, they reveal their deepest secrets, confront and console one another and share plenty of laughs. But how will they cope when a new crisis strikes?

Useful websites

Anxiety:

www.anxietyuk.org.uk
www.supportline.org.uk
www.socialanxietysupport.com

Counselling:

www.britishpsychotherapyfoundation.org.uk/
www.counselling-directory.org.uk

Mental health:

www.mentalhealth.org.uk
www.mind.org.uk
www.moodscope.com
www.rcpsych.ac.uk (Royal College of Psychiatrists)
www.rethink.org
www.actionforhappiness.org
sane.org.uk
www.time-to-change.org.uk

Addiction – www.alcoholics-anonymous.org.uk
Alzheimer's – alzheimers.org.uk
Bereavement – www.cruse.org.uk
Bipolar disorder – www.bipolaruk.org.uk
Depression – www.depressionalliance.org;
PTSD – www.ptsd.org.uk
Suicide – metanoia.org; www.samaritans.org (08457 909090)
Tourette's – www.tourettes-action.org.uk

General health:

www.bupa.co.uk
www.childline.org.uk
www.netdoctor.co.uk
www.nhs.uk
www.patient.co.uk

Anxiety/stress related articles

Anxiety:

http://www.dailymail.co.uk/femail/article-2614530/The-midlife-crisis-anxiety-epidemic-Palpitations-constant-fear-crippling-panic-attacks-chronic-anxiety-wrecking-lives-generation-women-live-for.html (includes my own story)

http://www.newstatesman.com/2014/04/anxiety-nation-why-are-so-many-us-so-ill-ease

http://www.telegraph.co.uk/health/wellbeing/11046587/How-to-detox-your-life-beat-anxiety-through-meditation.html

http://www.theguardian.com/society/2013/sep/15/anxiety-epidemic-gripping-britain

http://www.dailymail.co.uk/health/article-32984/How-treat-anxiety.html

Panic attacks:

http://www.dailymail.co.uk/health/article-2156928/How-control-panic-attacks.html

http://www.huffingtonpost.com/julie-sacks/personal-health-_b_5673365.html

Insomnia:

http://www.theguardian.com/lifeandstyle/2014/apr/19/tips-to-combat-insomnia

Mindfulness:

http://www.theguardian.com/lifeandstyle/2014/jan/11/julie
-myerson-mindfulness-based-cognitive-therapy

http://www.psychologytoday.com/blog/urban-
mindfulness/201106/mindfulness-and-anxiety-interview-dr-
lizabeth-roemer

Depression:

http://www.nytimes.com/2014/08/16/opinion/depression-
can-be-treated-but-it-takes-competence.html

http://www.theguardian.com/commentisfree/2014/aug/20/
men-suffer-depression-anxiety

http://www.huffingtonpost.co.uk/jamie-flexman/depression-
mental-illness_b_3931629.html

Recommended reading

Anxiety:

The Feeling Good Handbook, David D Burns

Overcoming Social Anxiety & Shyness, Gillian Butler

Overcoming Insomnia and Sleep Problems: A Self-Help Guide Using Cognitive Behavioural Techniques, Colin A. Espie

Feel The Fear And Do It Anyway: How to Turn Your Fear and Indecision into Confidence and Action, Susan Jeffers

Creativity/Art therapy:

The Courage to Create, Rollo May

Art Therapy Exercises: Inspirational and Practical Ideas to Stimulate the Imagination , Liesl Silverstone

Art as Therapy, Alain de Botton and John Armstrong

Mindfulness and CBT:

Mind Over Mood: Change How You Feel By Changing the Way You Think, Anton T Beck, Dennis Greenberger and Christine Padesky

Full Catastrophe Living, how to cope with stress, pain and illness using mindfulness meditation, Jon Kabat-Zinn

Sane New World, taming the mind, Ruby Wax

Mindfulness, A practical guide for finding peace in a frantic world,

Mark Williams and Danny Penman

The Mindful Way Through Depression, freeing yourself from chronic unhappiness (includes Guided Meditation Practices CD), Mark Williams, John Teasdale, Zindel Segal and Jon Kabat-Zinn

Depression:

Shoot the Damn Dog, a memoir of depression, Sally Brampton

Depression, The curse of the strong, Dr Tim Cantopher

The Examined Life, how we lose and find ourselves, Stephen Grosz

The Unquiet Mind, a memoir of moods and madness, Kay Redfield Jamison

Sunbathing in the Rain, a cheerful book about depression, Gwyneth Lewis

Please also see my website, **www.thecreativepumpkin.com,** where there's more detail on several of these titles.

SR

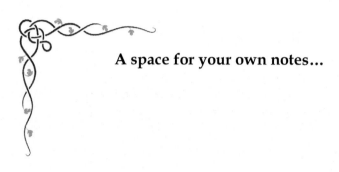

A space for your own notes...

127

130

Printed in Great Britain
by Amazon

42219862R00078